Everyday Food

Milk

Joyce Bentley

Chrysalis Children's Books

First published in the UK in 2005 by
Chrysalis Children's Books
An imprint of Chrysalis Books Group Plc
The Chrysalis Building, Bramley Road, London W10 6SP

ISBN 1 84458 181 0

British Library Cataloguing in Publication Data
for this book is available from the British Library.

Senior editor *Rasha Elsaeed*
Project editor *Debbie Foy*
Editorial assistant *Camilla Lloyd*
Food consultant *Brenda Alden*
Art director *Sarah Goodwin*
Illustrator *Molly Sage*
Designer *Ben Ruocco, Tall Tree Ltd*
Picture researchers *Sarah Stewart-Richardson, Veneta Bullen, Miguel Lamas*

Printed in China

10 9 8 7 6 5 4 3 2 1

Words in **bold** can be found in Words to remember on page 30.

Typography *Natascha Frensch*
Read Regular, Read Smallcaps and Read Space; European Community Design Registration 2003 and Copyright © Natascha Frensch 2001-2004 Read Medium, **Read Black** and *Read Slanted* Copyright © Natascha Frensch 2003-2004

READ™ is a revolutionary new typeface that will enhance children's understanding through clear, easily recognisable character shapes. With its evenly spaced and carefully designed characters, READ™ will help children at all stages to improve their literacy skills, and is ideal for young readers, reluctant readers and especially children with dyslexia.

Picture Acknowledgements
All reasonable efforts have been made to ensure the reproduction of content has been done with the consent of copyright owners. If you are aware of any unintentional omissions please contact the publishers directly so that any necessary corrections may be made for future editions.

Anthony Blake Photo Library: Tim Hill 5, Tony Robins 21B, Anthony Blake 23B; Bridgeman Art Library: Louis Pasteur (1822-95) in his Laboratory, 1885 (oil on canvas), Edelfelt, Albert Gustaf Aristides (1854-1905)/Musee d'Orsay, Paris, France, Giraudon 7; Chrysalis Image Library: Ray Moller 24T, 24B, 25; Corbis: Ted Horowitz 4, Bob Rowan 18, George W. Wright 19B, Craig Lovell 22, LWA-Dann Tardif 23T; Cephas: Vince Hart 21T; Frank Lane Picture Agency: W. Broadhurst 8T, Gerard Lacz 8B, M J Thomas 9, Peter Dean 14, 19T; Getty Images: Timothy Shonnard 26, Ray McVay 27; Holt Studios: Wayne Hutchinson 10, Nigel Cattlin FC, BC, 1, 11, 12, 13, 15, 16, 17T, 17B, Willem Harinck 20; Werner Forman Archive: 6.

Contents

What is milk?

Milk is a liquid that is made by female **mammals** to feed their young. It contains everything a young mammal needs to grow.

A baby **suckles** milk from its mother's breast for the first months of life.

Children and adults drink milk, too, as it is **nutritious** and tasty.

A dairy cow produces 6530 litres of milk a year.

Milk contains **nutrients** which are important for good health and growth.

Back in time

Milk is one of the earliest known food sources. A frieze dating back to 3000 BC shows milk being used as food. The Bible also talks about people drinking milk.

This carving shows an ancient Egyptian man milking a cow.

In 1856, Louis Pasteur invented a **process** called **pasteurisation** that killed harmful **bacteria** in milk. Bacteria can make people ill. Today milk is pasteurised to make it safe.

Pasteurisation was named after its inventor, Louis Pasteur.

All sorts of milk

There are many different animals that make milk. Cows, goats, sheep, buffalo, yaks and even camels all make milk for their young.

A newborn calf suckles milk from a cow.

A lamb suckles milk from a sheep.

Goat kids suckle from their mother.

We drink mainly cow's milk, which comes from a **dairy**. Cows that provide milk are kept on a dairy farm.

Cows and calves

Cows are **ruminants**. They live in fields and eat cereals, grass, cottonseed and hay. Nutrients in their food are used to make milk.

Even after the calf is **weaned**, the cow still makes milk that we can drink.

The cow makes milk to feed her calf. The calf suckles from the **teats** on the cow's **udder**.

A cow eats up to 100 kg of grass each day.

A cow makes milk for up to 11 months after giving birth.

The milking parlour

Cows are milked by machines in part of the dairy called the milking parlour. Before milking, the cow's teats must be washed.

Cows are often milked three or four times a day. The milking process does not hurt the cow.

The milking machine has four cups, which fit onto the teats and gently suck the milk out. Milk is pumped into storage tanks to keep it cool.

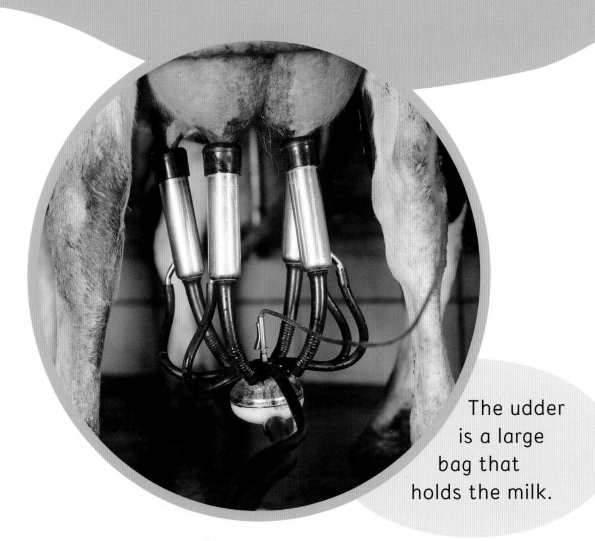

The udder is a large bag that holds the milk.

Storing and checking

Storage tanks keep milk at a temperature of 3°C/38°F. If the milk is too warm it will go **sour** before it reaches the shops.

Storage tanks have **thermometers** to ensure milk is kept at the right temperature.

The milk is checked, then pumped in to **refrigerated** lorries, called tankers, and driven to a **processing plant**.

A cow can produce over 24 litres of milk a day.

Tankers are designed to keep milk at the correct temperature.

Preparing milk

Milk is treated by pasteurisation to remove harmful bacteria. Milk contains cream. When it is **skimmed** or **semi-skimmed** some or all of the cream is removed to make it lighter.

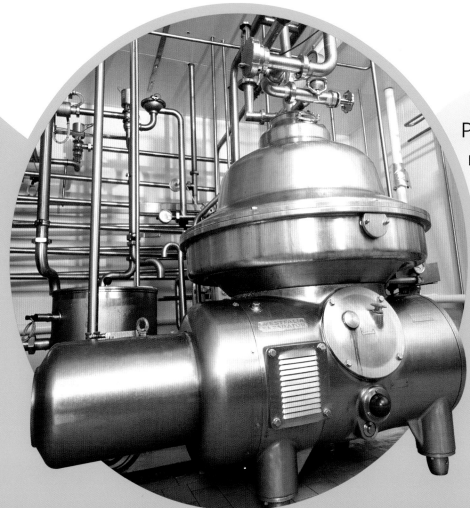

Pasteurised milk is heated to 72°C/161°F to kill all bacteria.

If cream is not removed then it is called whole milk. **Homogenisation** is a process that mixes the cream evenly throughout the milk.

Milk is pumped into containers.

Milk is labelled and sealed to keep it fresh.

Getting to you

It takes two days for milk to get from the cow to the shops. Lorries take the milk to supermarkets and shops where it is stored in fridges.

Fresh milk is available every day at shops and supermarkets.

Skimmed, semi-skimmed and whole milk are sold in different coloured containers.

Some dairies deliver the milk locally on **milk floats**. They leave the milk on people's doorsteps every morning.

Milkmen also deliver eggs, cheese and other **dairy products**.

Milk is a food!

You can drink fresh milk on its own, but it can also be used to make dairy products. Cheese, cream, butter and yoghurt are all made from milk.

Fresh milk tastes delicious straight from the fridge.

Pancakes are made with milk, eggs and flour.

Soufflés, quiches, puddings and pancakes are all made from milk. Cheese and yoghurt can be flavoured with **herbs**, fruit or nuts.

Milk is the main ingredient in all these dairy products.

Everyone loves milk

Most countries have cows or other animals that produce milk. Many countries have their own special recipes made with milk from local animals.

This Nepalese woman is milking a yak.

Ice cream is made from milk and cream, with different flavours added.

In Nepal people make cheese and butter from yak's milk. In Cyprus they make halloumi cheese from sheep's milk.

Crème caramel, rice pudding and trifle are all made from milk.

A balanced diet

Milk is a complete food and so contains lots of nutrients. It is a rich source of **protein**, **vitamins** and **minerals**. We need these as part of a balanced diet.

Other foods rich in protein are meat, fish, beans and nuts.

Fruit and vegetables contain **carbohydrates** and provide lots of vitamins and **fibre**.

For a balanced diet, most of the food we eat should come from the groups at the bottom of the chart and less from the top.

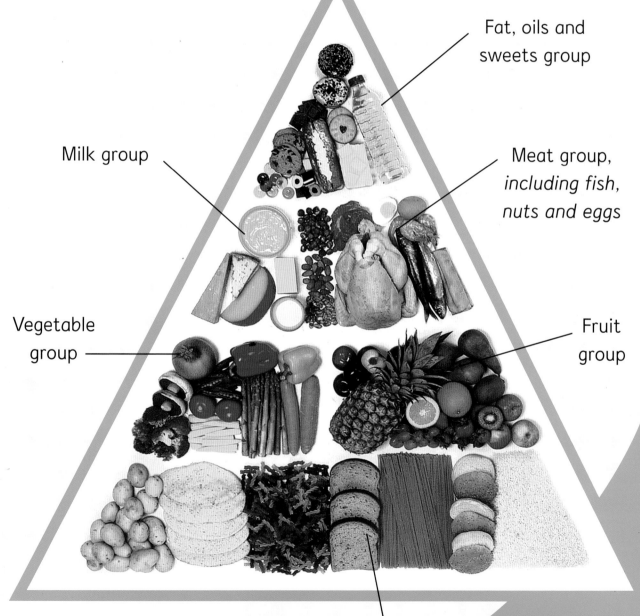

Fat, oils and sweets group

Milk group

Meat group, *including fish, nuts and eggs*

Vegetable group

Fruit group

Grain group, *including potatoes*

25

Healthy milk

We need protein for growth and repair.
Protein is especially important for children
as they are growing fast.

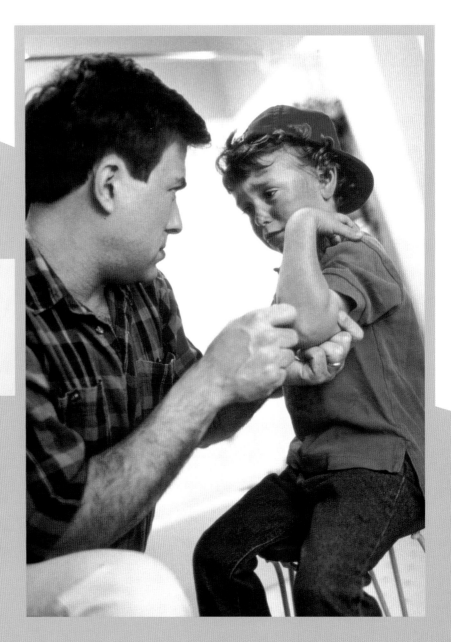

When you fall
and hurt yourself,
protein helps to
heal the wound.

Milk contains the mineral, calcium. It is good for healthy bones, teeth and muscles. Vitamins A, D and E in milk are needed for healthy skin and hair and to prevent illness.

Vitamins help children to grow up strong.

Banana milkshake

This shake is easy to make, delicious and really good for you!

Serves 2

Children in the kitchen must be supervised at all times by an adult.

YOU WILL NEED

- 1 banana
- 250 ml/9 fl oz milk
- 2 ice cubes
- 1 tablespoon honey
- 2 scoops ice cream

1. Blend all the ingredients (except the ice cream) in a food processor for one minute.

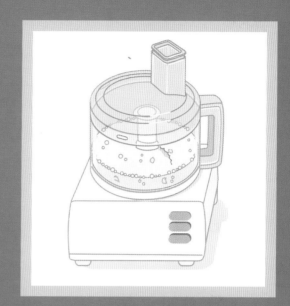

2. Pour the shake into two tall glasses.

3. Add a scoop of ice cream to each glass and serve!

Words to remembe

bacteria Tiny, living things that we cannot see, but can be harmful to us.

carbohydrates Nutrient the body needs for energy.

dairy A place where dairy products are made.

dairy products Milk and milk products such as butter and cheese.

fibre Material found in plants and grains that helps digestion.

herbs Plants that are used to flavour food.

homogenisation When the cream is evenly spread through the milk.

mammals Animals that feed their young on milk.

milk float A small vehicle that delivers fresh dairy products to your home.

minerals Nutrients the body needs for good health and to prevent illness.

nutrients Goodness in food that we need to stay healthy.

nutritious Foods that are healthy and good for you.

pasteurisation When milk is heated to a high temperature then cooled quickly to remove harmful bacteria.

process A series of actions that have an end result.

processing plant A place where food is treated and made ready for selling.

protein A nutrient that is needed for growth and repair.

refrigerated To be kept at low temperatures.

ruminants Animals that eat food, bring it back up and eat it again.

semi-skimmed Milk that has had some of its cream removed.

skimmed Milk that has had all of its cream removed.

sour When milk is no longer fit to drink as it has gone bad.

suckle To feed from the breast or teat.

teats The parts of the udder that the young suckle to get milk.

thermometer Something that measures temperature.

udder The sack under a cow that holds milk.

vitamins Nutrients the body needs for good health and to prevent illness.

weaned When a baby or young animal no longer needs milk from its mother and it is then encouraged to eat other foods.

Index